AF486790

Pa'lante

The Long Way Forward

Fourteen Principles for Living, Leading, and Becoming Whole

BY *ELVIS RIVERA*

TABLE OF CONTENTS

"And when it all eventually ceases to exist—the applause, the facades, the fleeting connections—what will remain is what we were. Who we were when no one was watching. When there was no reward to be won, no role to be played. Only the quiet truth of how we chose to be.

There will always come a time when we each must sit with the sum of our choices—the love we gave, the harm we caused, the kindness we offered when no one asked. In that moment, only what was real will matter.

So, live now—as the person you would hope to meet on your own deathbed. Live in such a way that when that hour arrives, your heart can rest easy, unburdened by the weight of what was left unsaid, unloved, or undone."

— Elvis Rivera

INTRODUCTION

There are lessons life teaches you gently and lessons it teaches you by force. The principles in this book came from the latter. They were shaped by migration, hardship, identity, responsibility, and the work of healing — long before success or leadership ever entered the picture.

My story begins in Guatemala, continues through Mexico, crosses into the United States in fear and uncertainty, and eventually finds ground in Houston and Minnesota. But geography is only part of that journey. The deeper truth is that everything I am was shaped by resilience long before I understood the word.

This book is not my memoir — that comes later.

This is the philosophy that made the memoir possible.

Move Forward Anyway

"Momentum doesn't come from certainty — it comes from choosing to take the next step even when you're afraid."

I learned early that progress rarely waits for permission. When my family fled Guatemala, nothing was promised. There were no maps, no guarantees, no certainty about where the next day would lead us. But what we did have was movement — one step at a time, even when fear traveled with us.

That instinct to keep moving, even without clarity, followed me into adulthood. Through homelessness. Through loss. Through reinvention in new cities. Through climbing in spaces not built for people who look like me. Every breakthrough in my life came not because I felt ready — but because standing still was no longer an option.

Reflection

Clarity is a reward
for movement, not a
prerequisite.

Application

- Take one small step today.

- Don't wait for certainty —
  build momentum instead.
  Trust that movement creates
  its own direction.

Know Where You Come From, Even When It Hurts

"Your roots aren't weights. They're anchors that keep you from drifting into a life that was never meant for you."

There are parts of our beginnings we wish we could rewrite. For years, I thought strength meant putting distance between myself and the places where my story began — the poverty, the fear, the instability, the things we survived but rarely talked about. I believed that in order to "make it," I had to become someone new.

But life has a way of reminding you where you come from.

Sometimes it's subtle — a smell, a sound, a phrase spoken in Spanish that pulls you back into memory. Sometimes it's a lesson your mother taught you without ever using words — the way she got up even when life pushed down hard. And sometimes it's more direct: the first time you look at your own children and realize the lengths your parents went to so you wouldn't inherit the same pain.

For me, I've had moments throughout adulthood where my roots showed up uninvited — in my leadership, my relationships, my sense of responsibility, and in the way I move through the world. It took me a long time to realize that distance doesn't heal what shaped you. Reflection does. Honesty does. Understanding does.

I come from a country scarred by civil war. I come from a family that faced circumstances many people don't survive. I come from a lineage of resilience, sacrifice, and stubborn hope.

And the truth is: acknowledging that didn't limit me. It grounded me.

Our beginnings are not curses — they're context. And context is power.

Reflection

We can't build a meaningful life by pretending we came from nowhere. The parts of our story that feel painful or complicated hold the blueprint to who we are becoming. Roots don't hold you back — they hold you steady.

Application

- Write down the three hardest truths about where you come from.

- Then write the three strengths those experiences gave you.

- Don't hide your roots — integrate them.

- Honor the parts of your story that kept you alive.

Build Community The Way You Needed Community

"Become the person you once needed. Build the spaces that once didn't exist for you."

Growing up, community wasn't always a stable thing for me. We had moments of support, moments of abandonment, and moments where strangers stepped in with more love than people who shared our blood. I learned early that community isn't about proximity — it's about presence.

As an adult, especially as a leader, I recognize clearly what was missing for me at various stages. I know what it feels like to walk into rooms where you are the only one. I know what it feels like to be underestimated, tokenized, or invisible. I also know what it feels like to be championed, mentored, believed in, and invited into opportunity.

So, I made a decision years ago — quietly at first, intentionally later:

I would build community the way I once needed it.

That commitment has shaped every role I've held. Whether in nonprofit work, corporate leadership, or public service, my instinct has always been to create belonging. To make space for people who learned to navigate systems that were never designed with them in mind. To ensure no one stood alone the way I once did.

Community doesn't build itself. It's carved day by day, conversation by conversation, choice by choice. And it starts with a simple question:

"What did I need when I was younger, and how can I offer that to someone else now?"

I didn't always have the community I needed growing up — but I can become that community for others. And that is the power of healing.

Reflection

When you build community from a place of lived experience, it's not theory — it's service. Community is an act of love, of memory, and sometimes of repair. The spaces we build today can heal the wounds we carried yesterday.

Application

- Think of a moment when you felt unseen — and make sure no one around you feels that way.

- Identify someone who needs what you once needed.

- Offer presence, not perfection.

- Be the bridge you once hoped someone would build for you.

Purpose Lives Where Pain And Talents Intersect

"Your purpose doesn't hide from your wounds — it grows through them."

For a long time, pain felt like something to outrun. It was heavy, confusing, and inconvenient — especially for someone trying to climb, excel, and "prove" themselves in spaces where vulnerability was treated like weakness. So, I did what many of us learn to do: I compartmentalized.

But purpose has a way of tapping you on the shoulder.

It doesn't ask for your permission, your timing, or your plan.

It shows up in moments when your pain and your gifts accidentally collide.

For me, this showed up the first time I was asked to speak publicly about being an immigrant. It showed up when someone pulled me aside and thanked me for saying something they had been carrying in silence for years. It showed up in the moments I realized my story wasn't just mine — it was a mirror for others, a doorway, a compass.

Pain taught me empathy.

Talent gave me voice.

Purpose emerged when I finally allowed the two to meet.

I used to think purpose was a destination — something you arrive at once you've healed. But the truth is my purpose grew out of the very things I once tried to bury. Not despite them — because of them.

Your pain is not your identity.

But it is your teacher.

And when you combine what hurt you with what moves you, something powerful happens:

You begin to live a life that feels aligned, not forced.

Reflection

Purpose is not about perfection — it's about alignment. When your gifts begin to serve the parts of you that once suffered, you stop performing and start becoming.

Application

- Write the three biggest pains that shaped you.

- Write your three greatest strengths.

- Draw lines between where they overlap — that's where purpose begins.

- Serve from your scars, not your wounds.

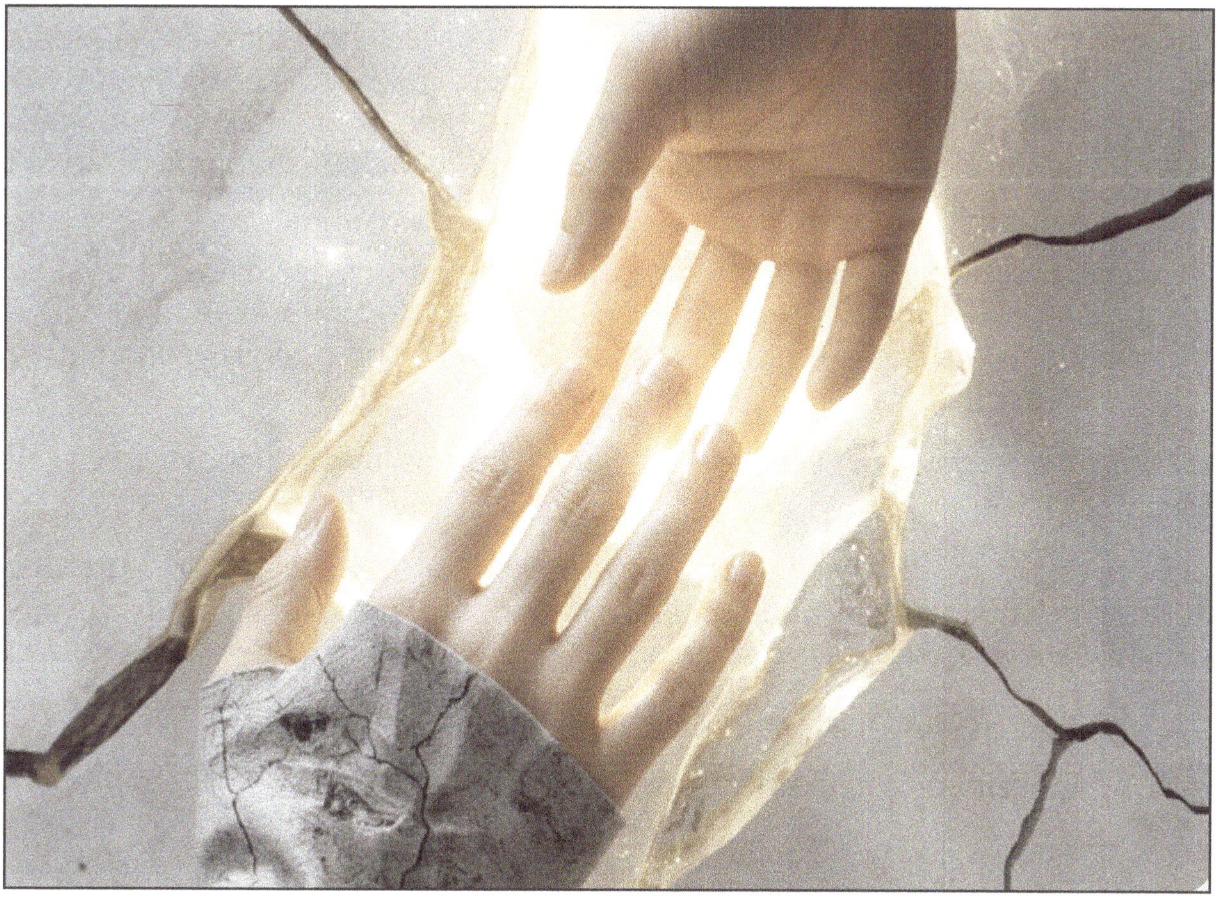

Service Is A Strategy, Not A Sacrifice

"Service is not what you lose by giving — it's what you gain by remembering why you're here."

Growing up in environments where survival took priority over everything else, service wasn't a word we used — but it was something we lived. My mother modeled it in ways I didn't understand until adulthood. She shared the little we had with families in worse situations than us. She offered help even when she had nothing to spare. To her, service wasn't a luxury — it was a responsibility, a way of honoring the fact that we, too, had relied on the kindness of strangers during the hardest parts of our journey.

As I got older and stepped into leadership roles, I saw how differently people viewed service. Some treated it as charity. Others saw it as an obligation. Many saw it as something that takes away from your time, your energy, your goals. But for me, service has always been a strategy — a way of shaping the world I want to leave behind.

Service has opened more doors for me than ambition ever has. It has introduced me to people I would have never met, built trust I could have never bought, and grounded me in a sense of purpose that kept me from losing myself in titles, roles, and recognition.

When I became involved in community work, boards, and advocacy, I realized something deeper:

Service aligns you with the people who are working toward a future you believe in. It keeps you connected to humanity. It clarifies your values. It reminds you who you are when no one is clapping.

Service is not a sacrifice — it is an investment.

And it pays dividends long after applause fades.

Reflection

Service is a strategy for staying human in a world that constantly pulls us toward self-preservation. It's a way of saying: "I haven't forgotten who helped me become who I am."

Application

- Identify one person or group you can support this month.

- Serve without expecting credit.

- Replace "What do I get?" with "Who do I become by doing this?"

- Let service be part of your long-term life strategy.

Identity Is Not A Barrier — It's A Compass

"The world may tell you to shrink, but your identity will always point you back to your true size."

There was a time when being a first-generation Guatemalan immigrant felt like a disadvantage in every room I entered. I carried the weight of my accent, my background, my story — not because it was shameful, but because the world taught me to minimize it. When you're the only one who looks like you, comes from where you come from, or carries your lived experience, you learn to blend in as a survival skill.

But blending in comes at a cost:

You lose your voice before anyone else ever silences it.

It took years for me to understand that my identity wasn't an obstacle — it was a source of direction. Every experience that made me different also made me valuable. My upbringing taught me resilience. My culture gave me community. My roots taught me humility, strength, and spiritual grounding. My story gave me clarity about what matters and what doesn't.

In corporate spaces, political arenas, and community rooms, the parts of me I once tried to quiet became the exact parts that guided my leadership. My identity sharpened my moral compass. It shaped my lens for justice. It informed how I advocate, how I lead, how I speak, and why I fight.

Identity is not something to "overcome."

It is something to honor and follow.

The world may try to tell you that you are too much, or not enough, or somehow outside the mold. But the truth is: your identity isn't in the way — it's the way forward.

Reflection

Your identity tells you what you stand for, what you will not tolerate, what you fight for, and where you belong. Don't shrink it to make others comfortable. Expand into it to make yourself whole.

Application

- Write three things your identity has given you.

- Ask yourself: "Where is my identity trying to lead me?"

- Stop minimizing what makes you different — highlight it.

- Use your lived experience as a leadership tool.

Ambition Means Nothing Without Healing

"You can outrun a lot in life — but you will never outrun what you refuse to face."

Ambition came naturally to me. Survival teaches you to hustle early. You learn to move fast, adapt fast, and push harder than the people around you because you understand what falling behind really means. Ambition becomes armor — a way of proving your worth, securing stability, and outrunning the parts of your past that still sting when you sit still long enough to feel them.

For years, I chased goals without ever stopping to ask:

"Why do I want this?"

"Who am I doing this for?"

"What am I ignoring in the process?"

Ambition gave me success — but healing gave me peace.

There came a point in my life when achievements no longer numbed the things I hadn't dealt with. The childhood wounds. The loss. The instability. The fear. The expectations I placed on myself. The expectations others placed on me. The pressure to be strong even when I was breaking quietly on the inside.

I realized that ambition without healing only builds walls — not foundations.

It wasn't until I slowed down and faced the unresolved parts of my story that I finally understood what I was really chasing: not titles, not applause, not recognition — but safety. Belonging. Worthiness.

Healing taught me that I was already enough. Ambition taught me how to build.

Together, they taught me how to rise without losing myself.

Reflection

Success built on unhealed wounds will always feel unstable. Healing gives ambition direction. It makes your goals meaningful instead of hollow. It allows you to climb without collapsing.

Application

- Identify a part of your story you avoid.

- Ask yourself: "What would happen if I stopped running from this?"

- Give yourself permission to rest.

- Pursue goals from wholeness, not fear.

Love And Leadership Start At Home

"How you lead at work is only impressive if the people you love can feel it too."

Leadership is often measured publicly — titles, promotions, influence, awards. But the older I get, the more I understand that real leadership shows up quietly, in the places where there is no audience and no applause.

I've held roles with big responsibility and bigger expectations. I've led teams, shaped decisions, and sat at tables where strategy, budgets, and policies determined the fate of entire communities. But none of those roles ever stressed me as much as the responsibility of showing up for the people in my home. Home is where your leadership is tested without the buffer of professionalism.

At work, you can compartmentalize. At home, everything bleeds together — your patience, your character, your wounds, your habits, your triggers. You can't hide behind credentials or performance reviews. Your people see you fully, flaws included.

I've had seasons where I led well out in the world but fell short in my own home — stretched thin, emotionally unavailable, exhausted from carrying too much. I've had moments where ambition outran presence, where goals overshadowed relationships, where I gave the best parts of myself to strangers and only the leftovers to the people who mattered most.

And I've had to learn — sometimes the hard way — that leadership without love is empty. Fatherhood taught me that. Partnership taught me that. Family taught me that. The most important leadership decisions I'll ever make won't be on a stage or in a boardroom — they'll be in how I speak to my children, how I show up for the people I love, how I repair after I get it wrong, how I hold space for those who count on me.

The world may celebrate what you do publicly, but the people you love will remember who you were privately.

Reflection

Real leadership begins with the people closest to you. Titles don't matter there — consistency does. Presence does. Love does. Your home is the first place you practice the kind of leader you claim to be.

Application

- Ask the people closest to you what they need more of.

- Commit to one daily act of presence with your family.

- Don't just lead publicly— lead privately.

- Repair quickly when you fall short.

Success That Doesn't Include Your Community Is Just Extraction

"Legacy isn't what you build — it's who rises because you did."

I've been in spaces where success is defined by individual achievement — the car you drive, the title you carry, the access you're given. But coming from where I come from, I can't separate my own success from the conditions that shaped me. I can't ignore the communities I grew up in, the people I watched struggle, or the barriers that once made the simplest opportunities feel out of reach.

Success that only benefits you is not legacy — it's isolation.

I learned that early through community work, through advocacy, through watching how policy impacts families like mine. But I learned it even more through firsthand experience — being the first in spaces where few, if any, people looked like me, spoke like me, or carried a story like mine.

When doors opened for me, they didn't open just for me. They opened because someone before me pushed, insisted, sacrificed, and created the possibility for someone like me to walk through. And with that comes responsibility — not to hold the door, but to widen it.

So much of my life has been driven by a promise I made to myself:

If I ever reached places that once felt impossible, I would make sure I wasn't the last.

That's why community work matters so deeply to me. That's why leadership is never just about the role — it's about the ripple. That's why I stay connected, stay grounded, stay accountable to the people and places that raised me.

Success without community is extraction.

Success with community is restoration.

Reflection

You cannot "make it" alone. And even if you could, the goal shouldn't be to escape your community — it should be to uplift it. Real legacy is measured in the lives touched by your rise.

Application

- Identify one door you can open for someone else.

- Ask yourself: "Who benefits from my success besides me?"

- Commit to sharing resources, not just stories.

- Remember: legacy is collective.

Lead With Compassion, But Don't Confuse That With Softness

"Compassion without boundaries is exhaustion. Boundaries without compassion are cruelty. Leadership is the balance."

For a long time, I believed compassion meant saying yes. Yes to more work. Yes to more responsibility. Yes to being the emotional anchor for people. Yes to carrying burdens that weren't mine. Growing up in environments where everything felt unstable, I learned early to absorb conflict, to soothe others, to make peace where peace didn't exist.

That conditioning followed me into adulthood.

Into leadership.

Into relationships.

Into every place where people expected strength and I delivered it at the cost of myself.

But compassion without boundaries isn't compassion — it's self-abandonment.

I realized this when I hit emotional burnout. When my yes became automatic. When people I cared about were unintentionally taking advantage of my capacity. When organizations rewarded my over-functioning but neglected my humanity. When I found myself depleted, resentful, and stretched thin in ways that weren't sustainable.

Learning boundaries was the turning point.

Boundaries didn't make me colder — they made me clearer. They allowed me to serve without losing myself. They showed me where compassion ends and responsibility begins. They taught me that saying no isn't a lack of care; it's an act of alignment.

And here's what I discovered:

People actually respect you more when your compassion has structure.

Leadership becomes stronger when love has limits.

And life becomes healthier when you stop rescuing people from the consequences of their own decisions.

Compassion should never require you to abandon yourself.

Leadership should never demand you disappear.

Reflection

True compassion
has boundaries. True
leadership has balance.
You don't have to
choose between being
kind and being firm
— the most effective
leaders are both.

Application

- Say no without apology or over-explanation.

- Ask yourself: "Is this my responsibility, or am I rescuing?"

- Practice compassion with clarity, not guilt.

- Protect your energy the same way you protect your commitments.

You Don't Escape Your Story — You Evolve It

"Growth doesn't erase your past. It transforms your relationship to it."

There were years when I tried to outrun my story — the trauma, the instability, the experiences that shaped me long before I had the language to describe them. I wanted distance. I wanted reinvention. I wanted a version of myself untouched by struggle.

But the truth is simple:

You don't escape your story. You evolve it.

For much of my life, I believed that success meant leaving the past behind — that ambition could bury pain, or achievements could rewrite memories. But instead, the past followed me into new cities, new roles, new relationships, and new versions of myself.

It showed up in how I reacted to conflict.

In how I loved.

In how I feared.

In how I hustled.

In how I protected myself.

It showed up in my drive to be stable, even when stability meant overworking.

It showed up in my instinct to help others, even when I was exhausted.

It showed up when I became a father and saw in my children the innocence I lost too early.

One day, I realized I could no longer outrun the boy who learned to survive chaos by becoming hyper-responsible. I couldn't keep pretending wounds weren't shaping my decisions. I couldn't continue believing that strength meant silence.

Facing my story didn't break me — it freed me. It allowed me to name what I carried. To forgive what needed forgiveness. To accept what happened and refuse to let it define my worth. To use my experiences with intention, not shame. I didn't escape my story — I reclaimed it. And in that reclamation, I became whole.

Reflection

Healing doesn't erase your story — it brings meaning to it. Your past becomes your wisdom, your power, your compass. You are not what happened to you. You are what you chose to become in spite of it.

Application

- Write one chapter of your life you've avoided revisiting.

- Ask what it taught you — not just what it took from you.

- Consider where your story is still influencing your choices.

- Transform the narrative by telling it with honesty and compassion.

Humility Makes You Teachable; Confidence Makes You Unstoppable

"Humility opens doors; confidence allows you to walk through them."

Humility came naturally to me because life humbled me early. Being undocumented, being poor, being displaced, being unseen — life didn't give me room for arrogance. I learned to listen. I learned to observe. I learned to earn respect without demanding it.

Yet for a long time, I mistook humility for smallness.

I thought speaking up was arrogance.

I thought taking space was disrespect.

I thought ambition had to stay hidden behind gratitude.

But life will eventually teach you that humility without confidence becomes self-erasure.

I remember sitting in rooms where I was the youngest, the only Latino, the only immigrant, or the only one with my lived experience. And even though I knew I belonged there, it took years before I believed it.

What changed me was realizing this:

Humility keeps you learning.

Confidence keeps you moving.

When I began speaking from experience instead of fear...

When I allowed myself to claim my expertise...

When I learned that confidence is responsibility, not ego...

Everything shifted. I started advocating more boldly. I started leading more assuredly. I started asking for what I deserved. I started creating opportunities instead of waiting for them. Humility kept me grounded. Confidence helped me rise. Together, they became the foundation of my leadership.

Reflection

Humility isn't thinking less of yourself — it's staying open. Confidence isn't thinking more of yourself — it's trusting what you've earned. Real growth requires both.

Application

- List one area where you need more confidence.

- List one area where you need to practice humility.

- Speak from experience, not fear.

- Let humility guide your learning and confidence guide your action.

Your Voice Is Your Leverage

"Silence protects systems, not people. Say the thing that sets someone free even if that someone is you."

For a long time, I learned to stay quiet. Growing up undocumented, you learn early that silence is safety. You learn to observe rather than speak. You learn that attention can be dangerous, that visibility can have consequences.

Later, in professional spaces, silence took a different shape.

I stayed quiet to fit in.

Quiet to survive politics.

Quiet to avoid being labeled "too much," "too passionate," "too outspoken."

Quiet because I believed my story didn't carry the same weight as those around me.

But every time I silenced myself, a piece of me stayed small.

I didn't fully understand the power of my voice until I used it to advocate for others — for my community, for young professionals of color, for immigrants, for families who lacked access, for people whose stories mirrored my own.

I realized my voice wasn't a risk — it was leverage.

It created movement.

It opened doors.

It shook the rooms that needed shaking.

It built bridges for people who had never been invited into certain spaces.

Using my voice wasn't about speaking loudly — it was about speaking truthfully. And every time I did, someone would tell me, "I've never heard anyone say that out loud."

That's when I understood: silence may protect comfort, but it doesn't create change.

Your voice is the most powerful tool you possess — not because of volume, but because of honesty.

Reflection

Your voice can heal, build, disrupt, elevate, and liberate. Use it with intention. Use it even when it trembles. Use it so others don't feel alone.

Application

- Speak up at least once this week where you'd usually stay silent.

- Share one truth you've been holding privately.

- Advocate for someone who hasn't found their voice yet.

- Remember: your story carries weight.

Pa'lante Is A Practice, Not A Slogan

"Forward isn't a direction — it's a decision."

Pa'lante is more than a word I grew up hearing — it is a philosophy, a rhythm, a way of being. It was the whisper my mother carried through every hardship. It was the mantra behind every risk my family took. It was the quiet prayer we lived through each impossible moment.

Pa'lante meant:

Keep going through fear.

Keep going through loss.

Keep going through uncertainty.

Keep going even when the world tells you to fold.

As an adult, it became more than cultural memory — it became my guiding principle. Through homelessness. Through grief. Through rebuilding. Through leadership. Through fatherhood. Through healing. Through reinvention after reinvention. Pa'lante was the thread that kept everything stitched.

People sometimes think forward means fast — but Pa'lante taught me otherwise.

Forward can be slow.

Forward can be quiet.

Forward can be exhausted.

Forward can be shaky.

Forward can be a whisper instead of a roar.

But forward is forward.

It is a decision you renew daily — sometimes several times a day. A commitment to keep rising, to keep healing, to keep serving, to keep loving, to keep showing up for the life you're building.

Pa'lante isn't something you say — it's something you live. And it is the final principle because it ties all the others together. Every chapter in this book, every story in my life, every lesson I've learned... all of it comes back to a simple truth: Forward is the only direction I've ever known.

Reflection

Progress doesn't always feel like progress. But consistency will take you further than intensity. Forward is a choice, a practice, a way of honoring every version of yourself that fought to get you here.

Application

- Choose one thing today to move forward on — even by 1%.

- Celebrate small steps as real progress.

- Remember: Pa'lante is a lifestyle, not a mood.

- When in doubt, choose the next right step.

Conclusion

There's a moment in every person's life when standing still becomes more painful than stepping forward. When the familiar, even in its discomfort, can no longer justify its place in your story. That moment is where change begins — not with certainty, not with perfection, but with willingness.

Every principle in this book was shaped by seasons when moving forward felt impossible. Times when fear sat heavy in my chest. Times when identity felt confusing. Times when I was grieving, rebuilding, or trying to make sense of the world around me. Times when my mother carried our future in her hands. Times when I held my children and realized they were inheriting not just my strengths, but my scars.

Pa'lante isn't a motto. It's a practice. A discipline. A decision we recommit to each day — sometimes loudly, sometimes quietly, sometimes with confidence, sometimes with trembling hands. But always with intention.

You don't need the whole map to begin. You don't need the full plan to grow. You don't need to feel ready to take the next step. You only need to honor the truth that lives inside you and trust that forward — however small, however slow — is still progress.

My hope is that these principles become anchors for you the way they were for me. That they guide you in seasons of uncertainty. That they offer clarity in moments of doubt. That they remind you of your strength when you forget. And that they help you build a life aligned with who you are becoming, not the limitations of where you began.

Wherever you are, whatever you're carrying, whatever you're dreaming — Pa'lante. Siempre.

Acknowledgments

No one walks their journey alone, and this book is no exception. It exists because of the people, communities, and moments that shaped me long before I ever imagined putting these principles into words.

To my mother — your courage is the foundation of my entire life. Every sacrifice you made, every risk you took, every night you pushed forward when the world was falling apart — I carry that with me in everything I do. This book is yours as much as it is mine.

To my children — thank you for giving my life meaning beyond titles, roles, or recognition. You remind me daily of the importance of becoming someone worthy of your admiration and trust.

To my siblings and extended family — your love, struggles, and laughter have been threads in the fabric of my resilience. Our story is complicated, painful, and beautiful, and I'm grateful for the parts of it we've walked together.

To Minnesota's Latino, immigrant, and BIPOC communities — thank you for being my purpose. You have taught me what leadership truly looks like. You've shown me what collective power can accomplish and why service must remain at the center of everything.

To my mentors, colleagues, and the leaders who saw potential in me before I knew what to do with it — thank you for guidance, accountability, and belief.

To every educator, advocate, storyteller, and community builder who offered wisdom along my path — your examples shaped these principles long before I wrote them down.

And finally, to the reader — thank you for trusting me with your time and your heart. If one sentence in these pages helps you move forward with courage, clarity, or compassion, then this book has done its job.

About the Author

Elvis Rivera is a first-generation Guatemalan immigrant, speaker, community advocate, finance professional, and public servant whose life's work centers on resilience, identity, and whole-life leadership. After surviving a dangerous migration to the United States, periods of homelessness, and the challenges of cultural assimilation, Elvis spent his adulthood transforming those experiences into purpose-driven leadership.

Professionally, he has served in roles across finance, community engagement, nonprofit governance, and statewide policy work. He has contributed his perspective in spaces where organizations, foundations, and leaders come together to discuss equity, entrepreneurship, and efforts to close the racial wealth gap. His work spans boardrooms, community spaces, and public institutions — all guided by the same core belief: service is a responsibility, not a title.

Elvis is also a storyteller. His writing blends lived experience with practical wisdom, offering a framework for healing, purpose, and forward movement. Pa'lante: The Long Way Forward serves as the philosophical foundation for his forthcoming memoir.

He lives in Minnesota, where he continues to champion immigrant voices, BIPOC communities, small business development, youth empowerment, and ethical leadership. Through his speaking, writing, and service, Elvis remains committed to one mission: helping others grow, heal, and move forward.